AF673303

SMART BRAIN RIGHT BRAIN

The Principles of Art

Om KIDZ
An imprint of Om Books International

First Published in 2021 by

Om KIDZ | Om Books International

Corporate & Editorial Office
A-12, Sector 64, Noida 201 301
Uttar Pradesh, India
Phone: +91 120 477 4100
Email: editorial@ombooks.com
Website: www.ombooksinternational.com

Sales Office
107, Ansari Road, Darya Ganj
New Delhi 110 002, India
Phone: +91 11 4000 9000
Email: sales@ombooks.com

Author: Swayam Ganguly
Editor: Nandita Bhardwaj
Art & Design: Anshuman Pandey, Gaurav Bhandari, Harish Arya

ISBN: 978-93-5276-853-0

Printed in India

10 9 8 7 6 5 4 3 2 1

CONTENTS

1. Introduction

Imagine that you are drawing a spaceship. First, you have to decide where you will place the spaceship on the page. Once your spaceship has been sketched, you have to choose how far the planets will be placed from the spaceship that is flying towards them. You also need to highlight that your spaceship is in movement, and so you will have to draw a few lines to show that it is travelling full steam ahead. Then, as you love stargazing, you will draw a shooting star. Now add colour. Lo and behold! You have created your very own artwork. You have also used some of the **Principles of Art** without even realising that you have done so.

2. Principles of Art

There are a few common rules that most works of art follow. This set of rules, also called principles of art, explain how the elements of art (line, colour, shape, form, value, space and texture) are used in an artwork for it to look complete. These principles are the tools to create art, study it, as well as judge it.

The seven principles of art are:

Symmetrical

Asymmetrical

Radial

Balance

Contrast

Movement

Emphasis Dominance

Rhythm

Pattern

Unity and Variety

POCKET FACT

The principles of art can help us understand whether a painting is successful, and if it is complete or not.

3. Balance

Balance is about where you place each object in the artwork. It is important to know how the elements are distributed on the canvas making the painting proportionate and well-composed. If there is an imbalance in the painting, it will cause discomfort to the person viewing it.

Balance is maintained in a painting by placing objects according to their visual weight

Horizontal Axis

Vertical Axis

How does one balance a painting?

A painting is said to be balanced if one half of the painting has the same visual weight as the other half. Visual weight refers to the impact each element in the artwork will have on you when you view the painting. Visual weight balances around an axis (an invisible line on the page) in an artwork. If the axis is horizontal, the visual elements balance on both sides of the axis. If the axis is vertical, the visual elements balance from top to bottom.

A work of art with perfect balance

What are the forms of balance?

Balance has three forms: symmetrical, asymmetrical and radial.

Symmetrical

Asymmetrical

Radial

1. Symmetrical Balance: When the composition is split in half and both sides of the composition have the same elements in the same position just like a mirror-image, or the two sides of a face it is known as **Symmetrical Balance.**

POCKET FACT

Research has found that learning and practising art helps in reading and in maths.

Symmetry can be further divided into Horizontal Symmetry and Approximate Symmetry. If the line passes through the pattern from right to left, hence dividing the pattern into equal halves, it is **horizontal symmetry.**

Horizontal Symmetry

Approximate Symmetry

Approximate symmetry means that the composition is nearly the same on both sides.

POCKET FACT

Your face is an example of symmetrical balance.

2. Asymmetrical Balance: Here, the composition is balanced by contrasting any one of the elements of art. For example, there might be a large object on one side of the composition that is balanced by a small object on the far side.

Asymmetrical Balance

3. Radial Balance: In radial symmetry, the elements are distributed equally around a central point, just like the spokes that circle the hub in a bicycle tyre or leaves around a central node.

Radial Balance

4. Contrast

Contrast is the difference between the elements of art in a composition. This is done in such a manner that each element is made stronger in relation to the other. When placed next to each other, contrasting elements grab the viewer's attention immediately. Contrast makes art more exciting and interesting.

Artists use contrast to make their art more exciting. Contrast can be achieved through colour

Contrast in a painting can be achieved by mixing any of the elements of art. If complementary colours (the colours that create the strongest contrast like red and green) are placed side by side, it is an example of contrast. Negative and positive space is also an example of contrast.

Depending on the kind of drawing that you are making, you have to decide how much space you would like between the elements in your drawing. The space which is unused in your drawing is known as **negative space**. The space that the objects in your drawing occupy is known as **positive space**.

Negative and positive space is also an example of contrast

POCKET FACT

Artists use contrast to show the difference between two things, or to make something stand out.

Contrast can be further divided into four parts:

Value Contrast shows the difference between hues or shades of a colour. Value contrast is the relationship between a light area and a dark area.

Intensity Contrast is the difference between a pure colour (primary colour) when placed beside a mixed colour (secondary or tertiary colour).

Value Contrast

Intensity Contrast

Temperature Contrast highlights the difference between warm and cool colours.

Temperature Contrast

Size Contrast

Size Contrast brings out the difference between large and small objects.

Contrast can also come in many forms like:

Colour Contrast: A contrast between light and dark or bright and dull colours.

Colour Contrast

Shape Contrast

Shape Contrast: A contrast between different shapes (rectangles and circles).

Texture Contrast: A contrast between smooth and rough texture in an artwork.

Texture Contrast

Interval Contrast

Interval Contrast: This type of contrast highlights the difference in the same area after a gap in time.

5. Emphasis/Dominance

Emphasis, a principle of art, highlights a certain area, object or element in a composition

A drawing, or a painting, is like a story sometimes. Just like a good story, a painting can have a hero. This main character does not have to be a person. An object in the painting, or an area in it can also be the main character of the painting or drawing.

But how do you decide what the main character in your painting will be? How will you get your viewer to look where you want them to, in your drawing or painting?

The answer is by using **emphasis**.

POCKET FACT

Emphasis is also known as focal point.

Emphasis is a way of using the elements of art to highlight a certain area, object or element in a composition for it to stand out and capture the viewer's attention immediately. An artist does this normally by using contrast, but other features like placement, size or colour may also be used to highlight.

Emphasis is also known as the focal point

The emphasis, or dominance, is achieved when there is one main feature and the other elements are secondary or subordinate to it. For example, the smaller elements will merge into the background while the larger elements will come to the front. This will bring about unity, which is important in the composition of your artwork.

When smaller elements merge into the background and one large element gains importance, emphasis is gained

How do you create emphasis?

By using colour

Look at the picture below. The single green parrot has been placed with grey birds and is clearly the focal point because of a strong contrast of colour, as well as being of a different shape from the other birds. It has also been isolated from the rest of the group.

There are three ways you can use colour contrast to add emphasis in art:

1. Complementary colours are placed opposite each other on the colour wheel because they are opposite or complementary to each other by being different in hue. Examples are red/green, blue/orange, and yellow/violet. They attract the viewer's eyes to a focal point when placed alongside one another.

2. A colour that is found in only one spot in the artwork is called an isolated colour. This stands out visually as it does not match with the rest of the colour scheme of the composition.

3. Absent colour is similar to isolated colour, but it is a single colour in an almost colourless artwork. The artist emphasises that only one object is in colour in the artwork.

By isolating objects

You can use isolation to add emphasis to your art. If you place an object of emphasis outside its group, your viewer is sure to notice it.

By using placement

A viewer's eyes are normally attracted towards the middle of a painting. If you place important objects or people near the centre of your artwork, it adds to their emphasis.

By making an element stand out

You can also create emphasis by making one element stand out because it is so different from the others. By doing something unexpected or unusual, you are creating emphasis.

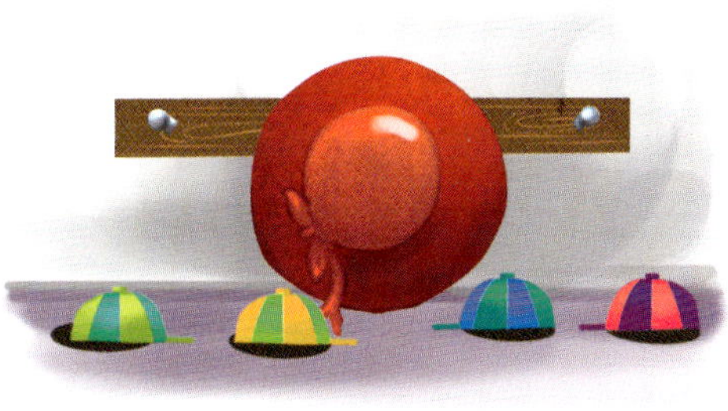

By using contrast

Apart from colour, the other two elements of art that help create emphasis through contrast are value and texture. If you use texture in just one spot, you can attract the viewer's attention. Also, bright colours are attractive. Road signs and traffic lights are brightly coloured to grab our attention.

6. Movement

Movement is the result you get when you use the elements of art in such a manner that it creates a feeling of motion, or a sense of action, in the artwork.

Movement in art is dependent on the other elements and principles of art. Rhythm, line, colour, balance and space play a major role to show movement in an artwork.

Movement, a principle of art, is used to create an interest in the painting

How do you create movement?

Remember that to show movement, or action, you cannot move your paints and colours physically in your artwork. So, what do you do? You will have to use the elements of art in such a way that it gives an illusion of movement or suggests that the objects are moving. Movement adds excitement, drama, and an interest in the composition.

Look at the picture below. Movement has been expressed in the most perfect and wonderful way with the help of the wind, the effect of which has been created by using elements of art like lines, colours and rhythm.

Movement in the above painting has been created by using elements of art, namely, lines, colours and rhythm

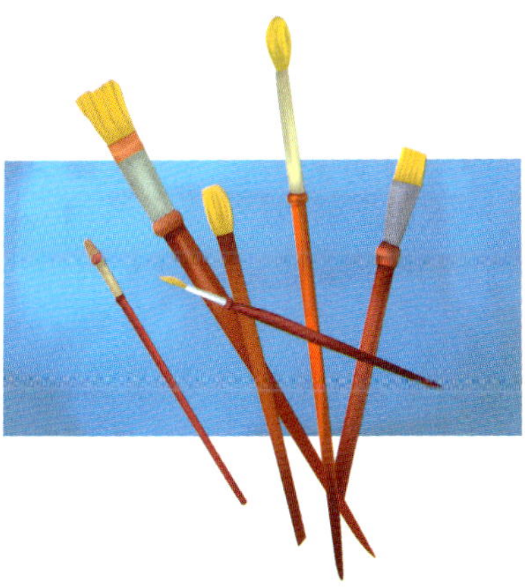

POCKET FACT

Movement is the path our eyes follow when we look at a work of art.

7. Pattern

Pattern is an important principle of art that deals with the visual arrangement of elements in a way that is repetitive, yet uniform. Through repetition, anything can be turned into a pattern in art. Examples of classic patterns are spirals, weaves and grids.

Pattern

There are two basic types of pattern in art: Natural Pattern and Man-made Pattern.

Natural Pattern: Natural pattern in art is inspired from nature, like the shape of a leaf and the branches of a tree, the structure of a crystal, the spiral of a shell, and the patterns on animals, fish and insects.

Natural Patterns

Man-made Pattern: Man-made pattern in art is used to create structure and to decorate. It is created by the artist through lines and shapes within the artwork.

Here are some patterns created by using the different elements of art:

Pattern through texture

Pattern through colours

Patterns through shapes

POCKET FACT

In pattern, we repeat visual elements like line, colour, shape, texture, value or image in such a way that the total effect of a work of art is united. This also creates rhythm and increases visual excitement.

8. Rhythm

In art, rhythm suggests movement or action. Like musical rhythm has a beat that is repeated, visual rhythm is created by repeating shapes (a pattern), colours and lines. Examples of visual rhythm are rows of windows and columns in architecture. Books in bookshelves and tiles on the floors are examples of rhythm in daily life. Rhythm provides a path for the viewer's eye to follow.

How do you create movement with rhythm?

Rhythm is created when the elements of art are repeated to create a feeling of movement or action.

There are three types of rhythm in art:

Regular Rhythm

This happens when elements similar in size or length are repeated at regular intervals.

Regular Rhythm

Progressive Rhythm

Progressive Rhythm

When you repeat elements but change the size or colour as they get repeated. For example, when building blocks are arranged from smallest to largest, and spirals.

POCKET FACT

Rhythm is different from pattern as it depends on variety, whereas pattern depends on consistency.

Flowing Rhythm

This happens when curvy positive and negative shapes and wavy lines are repeated.

Flowing Rhythm

Rhythm in art and music

Rhythm in art is related to rhythm in music. When you are listening to an upbeat pop song, the way the music notes are arranged creates a certain kind of pattern that you respond to in a natural way. For example, it makes you want to dance. It's the same way with rhythm in art.

Painting with an effective use of Rhythm

POCKET FACT

Rhythm in art is like the rhythm of music, but instead of notes and sounds, we use colours and shapes.

9. Unity and Variety

Variety

Unity

The basic difference between unity and variety is perfectly illustrated by the picture above.

In unity, the same colours are used in an artwork, but in variety, different colours are used.

Variety means that the objects in an artwork are of different sizes but in unity, the objects have the same size.

POCKET FACT

It is important to know that a great painting does not have to have the use of all the principles of art. In fact, most of the great paintings only use a few of the principles.

Unity

When all the elements in the painting fit comfortably and do not compete for attention is when unity is achieved. That is, all the elements and principles of art come together to create an image that is pleasing to the eye and the theme of your work is communicated clearly.

Unity is achieved when everything looks as if it belongs together

No matter what art style you are using, everything should look as if it belongs together. Unity breaks when even one element or principle of art is out of place. A good idea is to get an artist friend to evaluate your painting to check if anything feels out of place.

Variety

Variety means using differing qualities of the visual elements in a composition. For example, a painting with variety will have different colours being used and the objects in the painting will be of various sizes. Variety is used to break the monotony or repetition in a work of art by creating visual interest. You can create variety with change, contrast or by using elaborate elements. The image of different fruits and vegetables is an example of variety.

Here are some more examples of variety through the use of different elements of art:

Variety of colours

Variety of shapes

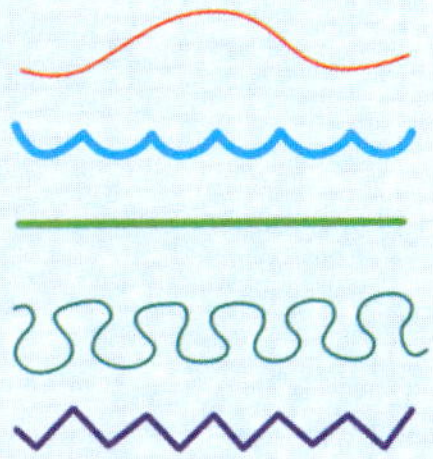

Variety of lines

Variety of sizes

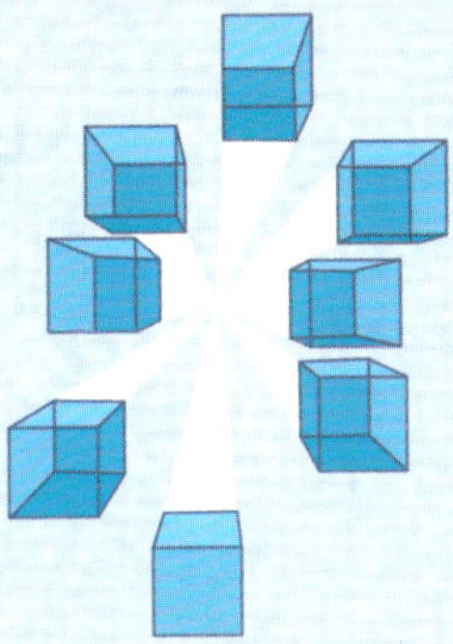

Variety of perspectives

Variety of textures

POCKET FACT

Too much unity creates monotony, and too much variety creates chaos. You need both for a good artwork in the form of a balance between unity and variety.

10. The Rules of Composition

There are no strict rules in terms of composition. Rather, they are age-old concepts that help a composition. The four famous concepts are:

- The golden ratio
- The rule of odds
- The rule of space
- The rule of thirds

The golden ratio is 1:1.62, or the ancient Greek ideal of a rectangle. Even bank cards use it.

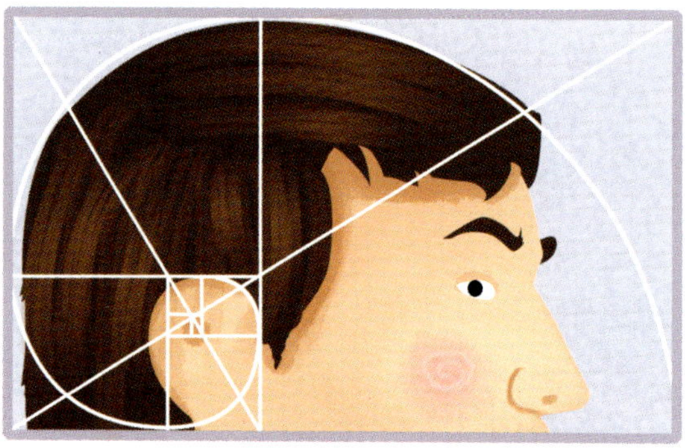

According to the rule of odds, 3 and 5 usually look more appealing than 2 and 4.

The rule of space highlights the fact that where there is empty space on a canvas, we imply movement towards it. This can be brought about by leaving open space in the direction the eyes are looking towards in a painting or by putting open space in front of the subject rather than behind it to suggest movement in that direction. So, if you have a train, boat, horse, car or a runner, you would put that empty space ahead of them to bring out that feeling of movement.

In the rule of thirds, a canvas is divided into horizontal and vertical lines in thirds and this is where the main elements of the painting should be placed.

POCKET FACT

Having an odd number of things in a composition means that the eye and the brain cannot pair them up or group them easily. There is always one thing that is leftover, and this forces the eyes to move across the composition.

1. Select a word from the word bank to fill in the blanks.

Word Bank:

(a) focal point (b) unity

(c) balance (d) pattern

1. Visual __________ is achieved when all parts of a composition appear to have equal weight.

2.__________ in a work is obtained by repeating colours and shapes when all parts of a design work together as a team.

3. Another term for centre of interest is __________.

4. Lines, colours, or shapes repeated over and over in a planned way is __________.

2. Identify the principles of art in the illustrations given below:

3. With the help of the key colours complete the composition of art below.

Key Colours:

1. dark blue
2. light blue
3. brown
4. light brown
5. green
6. yellow

GLOSSARY

Stargazing	to observe the stars
Organise	arrange systematically
Analyse	study
Imbalance	lack of proportion or relation between corresponding things
Saturated	holding as much as can be absorbed
Dominance	power and influence over others
Subordinate	lower in rank or position
Implied	suggested but not expressed directly
Rendered	to make
Respond	react
Underlying	a layer under something

ANSWERS

Page 30.

1. Activity

1. balance
2. Unity
3. focal point
4. pattern

2. Activity

1. Symmetrical Balance
2. Asymmetrical Balance
3. Regular Rhythm
5. Radial Balance
6. Natural Pattern
7. Rhythm